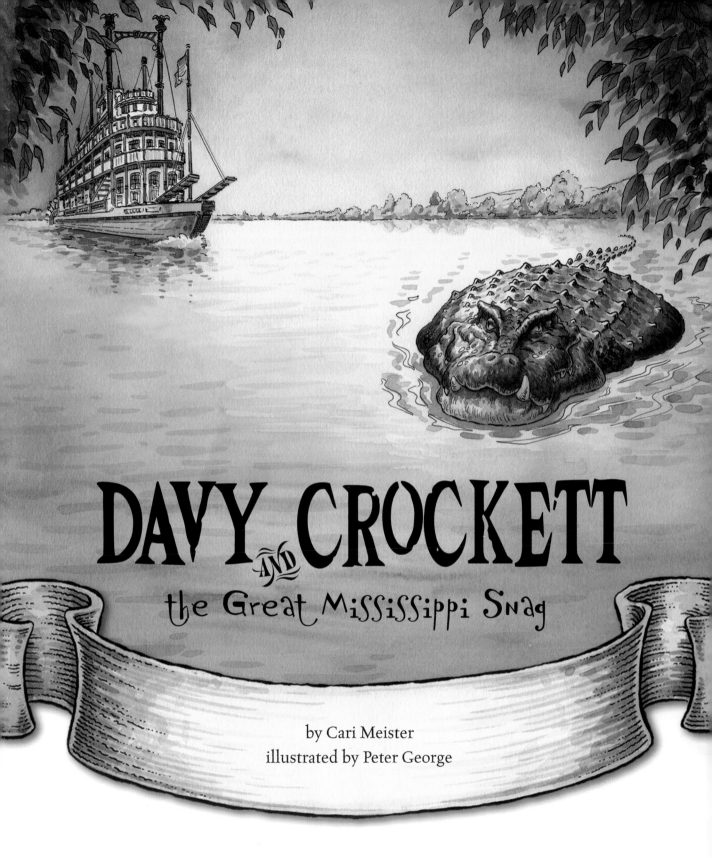

DAVY CROCKETT
and the Great Mississippi Snag

by Cari Meister

illustrated by Peter George

PICTURE WINDOW BOOKS
a capstone imprint

DAVID CROCKETT— the Man

David Crockett was born in 1786 in Tennessee. At that time Tennessee was still mostly wilderness. Folks who lived there hunted and fished for food. They lived off the land.

David spent his childhood hunting and fishing. Even as a boy he was a great hunter. David grew up and married twice. He had six children. He served in the U.S. Congress. David died fighting at the Battle of the Alamo in 1836. He was a popular man in his own time. But it wasn't until after his death that he became the legend that we know and love today.

Some time ago the West was as wild as a headless chicken on
a Saturday night. And into that wilderness, in the backwoods of
Tennessee, a baby was born. His name? Davy Crockett!

Well, Davy wasn't exactly born. He fell from the sky with a rifle
on his back and a coonskin on his head. He had a grin that was
fixin' to win the world over.

By the time Davy was 9 years old, he had killed more varmints than any other Tennessee man. It was said that he could grin down a bear. Why, he could even whip his weight in wildcats!

Yesiree, Davy Crockett was special. And by special, I mean *mighty* special. It's a darn tootin' fact that Davy Crockett once saved the world from crashin' with Halley's Comet.

Davy was doggone smart too. He served in the 21st Congress of these here United States. But there's no use beatin' the devil around the stump. Those are tales for another day.

Today I'm gonna tell you about the time Davy battled a fierce river beast feared by all.

Now, before roads criss-crossed the land, Mississippi River
business was big. Goods and people traveled up and down
"Old Muddy" like a giant highway. And the gators that lived in
the river were none too happy neither. They didn't like movin'

out of the way every time a steamer passed by. So late one August, those gators gathered together to plot revenge. They chose the most terrifyin' gator that ever lived to carry out that revenge. His name was Snag.

Snag was longer than two steamers put together. And his teeth? They were sharper than the farmer's wife's carving knife. But it was his eyes that made your blood curdle. Those great big yellow eyes.

It was said that one look from Snag, and you were done for.
He didn't even have to use his teeth—but he did. He chomped
through steamers like they were soda crackers!

For weeks Snag
had his fun. He
chomped up boats
and swallowed
the goods.

He scared the
molasses out
of everyone!

Snag was feelin' pretty high and mighty. So he moseyed over to the farms and gulped down all of the animals.

Well, when Davy heard about ol' Snag, he was stormin' mad. "Somethin's gotta be done," he said. "That sly Snag has sunk more boats than old grandaddy Neptune. I don't reckon anyone but me can take on Snag."

Davy boarded the next rig headin' toward Snag. It was a steamer loaded with food and fireworks for a big Fourth of July celebration up river.

Everything was goin' mighty swimmingly for a while. There was no sign of big ol' Snag.

"He must've heard I was comin' and sunk to the bottom of the river," Davy said. "If he doesn't show himself by nightfall, I'll go lookin' for him."

Then all at once, the steamer jerked to a halt and …

CRASH! SMASH! CRASH!

"Murder and mercy!" shouted the crew. **"IT'S SNAG!"**

Sure enough, that mighty beast's head was stickin' right up through the ship's bow! His yellow eyes were gleamin'. He was madder than a hornet! That deck was torn to smithereens.

"You no-good hog swallower!" yelled Davy, breakin' Snag free from the deck.

Then that ol' coot let loose and came back toward the steamer
again at full speed.

"He's aimin' to sink us!" yelled the captain.

"Not while I'm on duty!" bellowed Davy. He jumped on that ol' gator like it was a buckin' bronco.

They flipped and flopped and crashed and smashed.

The steamer was in bad shape, and Davy knew it had to stay afloat. So he rode that gator away.

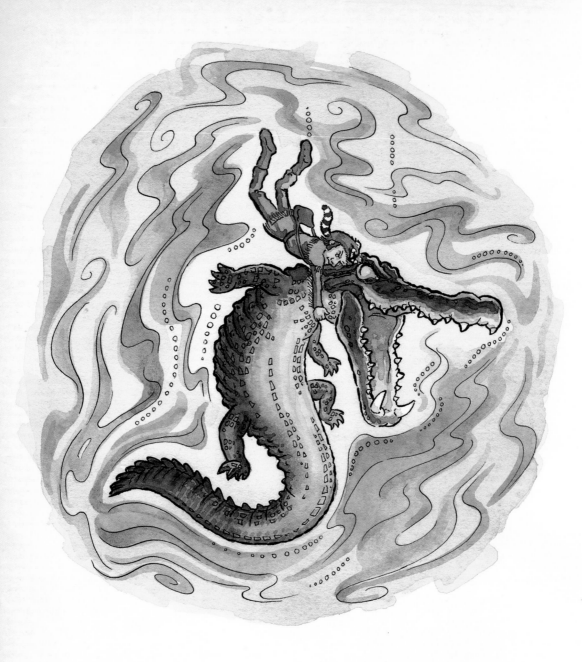

Now, Snag could hold his breath underwater for quite some time. But what he didn't know was that Davy could hold his even longer.

After wrestlin' underwater for six hours, Snag finally surfaced. He launched Davy onto the deck of the steamer. That made Davy boilin' mad!

Davy reached down and yanked Snag up onto the deck. His foot stomped on the beast's huge under jaw. His hands pushed on the upper jaw. Sure enough, he split that varmint apart as slick as a fence rail!

And do you know what came out of ol' Snag's belly?
Why, 214 pigs, 87 cows, 128 jars of applesauce, 22 barrels
of pickles, parts of four steamers, and nine live sailors.

AND BOY, WERE THOSE SAILORS HAPPY TO GET OUT!

The very next day was the Fourth of July. I'm told that it was the finest fandango Tennessee had ever seen. Davy Crockett himself led the dancin' and singin.' Even the president of the United States stopped by to dance a jig!

The American Frontier was wild land. Only the toughest folks survived. Some of their stories became the subjects for folktales. These stories were passed on, changed, and passed on some more. Davy Crockett became the hero of more books, movies, and songs than most. But why did the legend of Davy Crockett become so famous?

David Crockett was a hero in his time. People looked up to a man who had mastered the wilderness. Yet David was also smart. He was a leader in government, and he died fighting for his beliefs.

Over the years the legend of Davy Crockett grew. First there was the *Crockett Almanac*. A series of *Crockett Almanacs* were made from about 1835 to 1856. People all around the country read about Davy's heroic deeds on the frontier. After the almanacs, there were movies. Since 1909 more than 20 movies have been made about Davy Crockett.

In the 1950s Disney made a popular TV show about Davy. The show even had a song—"The Ballad of Davy Crockett." In the song Davy was called the "King of the Wild Frontier."

David Crockett the man lived more than 200 years ago. But Davy Crockett's legend lives on today because we continue to enjoy his heroic stories.

Learn More About Folktales

Although there are many different American folktales, each story contains similar pieces. Take a look at what usually makes up an American folktale:

hero—the main character of an American folktale is most often a hero with exaggerated abilities, or abilities that seem greater than they actually are

humor—most early American folktales are funny; the exaggerated characters and situations add to the humor

hyperbole—exaggeration; used in folktales to make the characters seem larger than life, almost magical

quest—a challenge; most early American folktales include a challenge that the main character faces; the challenge may include defeating a villain

slang—words and phrases that are more often used in speech, and are usually used by a certain group of people; common cowboy slang consisted of words and sayings such as "There's no use beatin' the devil around the stump," which meant there's no use avoiding a difficult task

Critical Thinking Using the Common Core

1. American folktales often include hyperbole, or exaggeration. Can you find some examples of hyperbole in this story? (Key Ideas and Details)

2. If you could retell a story from your past, what details would you include and why? Which common folktale elements could you use to make the story even more exciting? (Integration of Knowledge and Ideas)

Glossary

almanac—a book published yearly that has facts on many subjects

Battle of the Alamo—a battle on March 6, 1836, between Mexican and Texan troops at a mission church in San Antonio, Texas, called the Alamo; all of the Texans died, and the Mexican troops won the battle

Congress—the group of elected people who make laws for the United States

fandango—a big celebration or party

folktale—a traditional, timeless tale people enjoy telling

frontier—the far edge of a settled area, where few people live

jig—a lively dance with leaping movements

legend—a story handed down from earlier times; legends may be based on facts, but they are not entirely true

Neptune—the Roman god of freshwater and the oceans

revenge—an action taken to repay harm done

smithereens—small pieces

steamer—a steamboat

varmint—a wild animal

wilderness—an area that hasn't been disturbed by humans

Read More

Herman, Gail. *Who Was Davy Crockett?* Who was... New York: Grosset & Dunlap, an Imprint of Penguin Group, 2013.

Yomtov, Nel. *Defend Until Death!: Nickolas Flux and the Battle of the Alamo.* Nickolas Flux History Chronicles. North Mankato, Minn.: Capstone Press, 2014.

Thanks to our advisers for their expertise, research, and advice:

Elizabeth Tucker Gould, Professor of English
Binghamton University

Terry Flaherty, PhD, Professor of English
Minnesota State University, Mankato

Editor: Shelly Lyons
Designer: Tracy Davies McCabe
Art Director: Nathan Gassman
Production Specialist: Jennifer Walker
The illustrations in this book were created with pen and ink with watercolor wash.

Design element: Shutterstock: 06photo

Picture Window Books are published by Capstone,
1710 Roe Crest Drive, North Mankato, Minnesota 56003
www.capstonepub.com

Library of Congress Cataloging-in-Publication Data
Meister, Cari, author.
Davy Crockett and the Great Mississippi Snag /
by Cari Meister.
pages cm. — (Picture window books. American folk legends)
Summary: Davy Crockett battles Snag, a fierce gator, from destroying steamers along the Mississippi River. Includes bibliographical references.
ISBN 978-1-4795-5431-7 (library binding)
ISBN 978-1-4795-5448-5 (paperback)
ISBN 978-1-4795-5456-0 (eBook PDF)
1. Crockett, Davy, 1786-1836—Legends. [1. Crockett, Davy, 1786–1836—Legends. 2. Folklore—United States. 3. Tall tales.] I. Title.
PZ8.1.M498Dav 2015
398.22—dc23   2013050825

Printed in the United States of America
in North Mankato, Minnesota.
112014   008550R

Internet Sites

FactHound offers a safe, fun way to find Internet sites related to this book. All of the sites on FactHound have been researched by our staff.

Here's all you do:

Visit *www.facthound.com*

Type in this code: 9781479554317

Check out projects, games and lots more at
www.capstonekids.com

Look for all the books in the series:

Davy Crockett and the Great Mississippi Snag
John Henry vs. the Mighty Steam Drill
Johnny Appleseed Plants Trees Across the Land
Pecos Bill Tames a Colossal Cyclone